Gospel Hoarders

How Short-Term Missions Can Change the Way You Share the Gospel

RICK VIA with JACOB VIA

Foreword by Alvin Reid

WestBow Press
A DIVISION OF THOMAS NELSON

Copyright © 2012 Rick Via & Jacob Via

All rights reserved. No part of this book may be used or reproduced by any means, graphic, electronic, or mechanical, including photocopying, recording, taping or by any information storage retrieval system without the written permission of the publisher except in the case of brief quotations embodied in critical articles and reviews.

Scripture taken from the New King James Version®. Copyright © 1982 by Thomas Nelson, Inc. Used by permission. All rights reserved.

WestBow Press books may be ordered through booksellers or by contacting:

WestBow Press
A Division of Thomas Nelson
1663 Liberty Drive
Bloomington, IN 47403
www.westbowpress.com
1-(866) 928-1240

Because of the dynamic nature of the Internet, any web addresses or links contained in this book may have changed since publication and may no longer be valid. The views expressed in this work are solely those of the author and do not necessarily reflect the views of the publisher, and the publisher hereby disclaims any responsibility for them.

ISBN: 978-1-4497-5977-3 (sc)
ISBN: 978-1-4497-5976-6 (e)

Library of Congress Control Number: 2012912862

Printed in the United States of America

WestBow Press rev. date: 07/25/2012

—From Rick—
To Janet,
the love of my life and my greatest teammate

—From Jacob—
To my best friend, Keesha,
for being a godly, gorgeous, excellent wife and mother

Contents

Foreword ix
Introduction xi
Chapter 1: Why Short-Term Missions? 1
Chapter 2: Answering Common Objections 7
Chapter 3: Choosing Your Mission 17
Chapter 4: Forming Your Team 25
Chapter 5: Sharing the Gospel Cross-Culturally 33
Chapter 6: Managing Logistics 49
Chapter 7: Spiritual Preparation 63
Chapter 8: A Movement among Us 73
Notes 81

Foreword

As I write I sit in a Starbucks in Cochrane, Alberta, Canada. It is springtime, but it gets so cold here they have electrical outlets in all the parking lots to keep car engines warm in the brutally cold winters. If you venture out in sub-zero temperatures, should you wear a really heavy coat or should you cover your hands and head?

The answer of course is simple: you do both! Likewise, today we need both career missionaries whom God calls to plant their lives, and short-term mission teams to come alongside them. I don't know about you, but I am so happy to live in the twenty-first century. I can get on a plane and in a day be halfway around the world. What an opportunity. Why would we not go, given the fact that we have the greatest message on earth (the gospel), the greatest commission ever given (Matthew 28:19-20), and the greatest opportunity in history to go to the ends of the earth?

I have led or been part of mission teams in four continents, including places such as Western Europe, the former Soviet Union, Southern Asia, and South Africa. This year I will be in Ukraine and Canada, and I personally hope to spend a good bit of the rest of my life overseas on short-term mission trips. I teach at a school that sends out scores of career missionaries and I also go on multiple short-term trips annually. I am part of a church that goes all over the world each year on such trips. For these reasons, I so love this book by my friends Rick and Jacob Via.

Gospel Hoarders will help you to plan and execute successful trips. It will be essential reading for every team of which I am a part from this day forward. Why should we go on trips? Read it and you will see. What about the questions people raise? They will be answered. You will gain valuable information to help form and lead effective trips that will provide sustainable, gospel-focused work for the glory of God.

This idea of short-term trips is not a small deal to me. My wife Michelle and I believed in the importance of our children getting out of the country and to major US cities from their early days. I took my son Josh to Chicago to do mission work when he was twelve. He went to Central America at age fifteen. He also went across Europe on a school trip at eighteen, and has been back to Chicago and to Manhattan on mission trips since. My daughter Hannah has been to four continents—North America (the US), Europe, Asia, and Africa—and she is only nineteen. Our children have been shaped by seeing so many nations.

Too many of us are *gospel hoarders*. It is time for the church to be gospel heralds to the nations. Never have we lived at such a time of opportunity. God is moving. Join the movement!

Alvin L. Reid
Professor of Evangelism and Student Ministry/Bailey Smith
Chair of Evangelism Southeastern Baptist Theological Seminary
Wake Forest, North Carolina

Introduction

When one of my sons was five years old, he worked hard on memorizing John 3:16. His plan was to quote it to me when I returned home from a trip. When I walked in the door, he came running to me and said, "Dad, I can quote a Bible verse!"

I looked at him and said, "Great, son! Let me hear it."

With great pride he started, "For God so loved the world that He gave His only *forgotten* son . . ."

My son did not know the difference between the word *begotten*, meaning unique or one of a kind, and the word *forgotten*.

The truth is, there are many places around the world where Jesus Christ is God's "forgotten" Son. He is forgotten in some places because of hostile governments and religious persecution. He is forgotten in other areas because of materialism and indifference. There are still countless villages and communities scattered across the globe that have no access to the gospel of Jesus Christ. There will never be enough full-time vocational missionaries and Christian workers to reach those areas, communities, and villages.

That is where the church (and your church) comes into play. Our churches are filled with people who could participate in a short-term mission project to a needy part of the world. God has given gifts, abilities, and resources to those in our churches that could be used in advancing the gospel all over the globe. It may be that your church or ministry could work beside an established mission or missionary and begin to invest in that mission or missionary's area long-term. It could also be that our Lord will enable you to start a new work in an area where there is no church, pastor, missionary, or Christian witness.

Now, you may be asking, "How could we possibly accomplish something like that?" Well, the reason for this book is to show you how. I want to help you explore the opportunities and possibilities of taking the gospel to a part of the world that Jesus Christ died to save. You, your church, your family, and your ministry have the tools and resources that God can use to impact lives for Jesus Christ outside the North American continent.

I was attending a Bible conference some time ago when a pastor shared the following account. He had been conducting an evangelistic mission in Kenya, East Africa with a small team. They had been sharing the love of Jesus Christ in a remote village outside of Nairobi. At the end of the day, they were loading up their vans to leave the village. This pastor noticed an elderly man leaning against a mud brick building and felt compelled to speak to him. In the process of their conversation he was able to lead the elderly Kenyan man to faith in Jesus Christ. After rejoicing with the man, the pastor turned to leave when the man stopped him.

"I have a question to ask you before you leave," he said. "All of my life I have waited to hear this message. What took you so long to get here?"

There are millions of people all over the world who are still waiting to hear a clear presentation of the gospel of Jesus Christ. The problem is not that they do not want to believe. The problem is they have not been told so that they can believe!

> How then shall they call on Him in whom they have not believed? And how shall they believe in Him of whom they have not heard? And how shall they hear without a preacher? And how shall they preach unless they are sent? (Romans 10:14-15)

Scripture teaches that to whom much is given much is required (Luke 12:48). Americans have more resources, more churches, more Bibles, more Christian training, and more access to the gospel than any other place in the world. Have we become gospel hoarders? Hoarding is defined as the act of accumulating possessions and carefully guarding them or hiding them. Is that what we have done with the gospel? How often do we share the gospel with someone? How many Bibles do we own that just sit around the house? Are our churches focused on reaching the lost, or do we hide inside our houses of worship with doors closed to the world? We are surrounded with Christian radio and TV stations, movies, bookstores, Bible studies, conferences, and so much more. These things can be great tools used by God. But in a world where social media is a part of our daily lives and there is a church on every street corner, how easy it is to take for granted the abundant access we have to the gospel? God has greatly blessed our nation and our churches. Therefore, we have a huge responsibility to share what God has given us with the rest of the world. In this book I hope to give you a place to start.

Whether you are a seasoned mission traveler or are just beginning to prepare for your first mission experience, I pray that the thoughts and insights in this book will be helpful as you prepare for your journey. I want to help you as you and your church undertake the process of forming your missional strategy. I know this may be a brand new endeavor for many, but through much prayer and planning, I believe we can make it a reality. So I invite you to read this book with an open heart and mind to the moving of the Spirit of God. It could bring an end to gospel hoarding in your church and the beginning of an exciting journey in changing the world!

My desire and purpose is this: To see every local church directly involved in sending and going.

Chapter One
Why Short-Term Missions?

> "The church began in power, moved in power, and moved just as long as she had power. When she no longer had power she dug in for safety and sought to conserve her gains. But her blessings were like the manna: when they tried to keep it overnight it bred worms and stank."
> ~ A.W. Tozer

Over the last thirty years, I have been a part of several disastrous short-term projects. Because of a lack in leadership, strategy, and preparation, I have seen more harm than good come from many mission trips. This can destroy the morale and determination of a pastor, a mission team, and an entire church. So, then, why try? Why not just let the full-time missionaries do the work? Because missionary work is crucial for the spiritual growth of the believer and the church around the globe. Consider the following reasons why, when executed properly, a short-term mission is an important part of touching the world with the gospel of Jesus Christ.

1. The Great Commission commands it. Whether short-term or long-term, our Savior has commanded us to go.

   And Jesus came and spoke to them, saying, "All authority has been given to Me in heaven and on earth. Go therefore and make disciples of all the nations, baptizing them in the name of the Father and of the Son and of the Holy Spirit, teaching them to observe all things that I have commanded you; and lo, I am with you always, *even* to the end of the age. Amen. (Matthew 28:18-20 NKJV)

2. A short-term mission can energize your church and can increase interest in giving more toward missions in general. When church members return home from ministry abroad, the enthusiasm they bring back can be contagious. It gives the whole church a sense of identity with the people to whom they have ministered.

3. Individuals who participate in a short-term mission come home with a deeper love for Jesus Christ and a greater compassion for the world. Their experience will truly change the way they share the gospel in their home, their workplace, and their community. Our goal is to develop mature, global-minded disciples, who accurately reflect the image of Christ. Short-term missions can play a large role in that development.

4. God uses many short-term mission trips to call people into full-time vocational missions. We have seen this take place in the lives of a number of families that were first exposed to foreign missions through one of our trips. As the Lord worked in their lives, they were called to serve full-time in areas including Uganda, India, Kenya, and Venezuela.

5. Vocational missionaries and mission organizations are always asking for churches and volunteers to come and help.

   And a vision appeared to Paul in the night. A man of Macedonia stood and pleaded with him, saying, 'Come over to Macedonia and help us.' Now after he had seen the vision, immediately we sought to go to Macedonia, concluding that the Lord had called us to preach the gospel to them. (Acts 18:9-10)

   Missionaries will never be able to accomplish their mission without additional help and support.

6. God can use our simplest attempts at missions and evangelism to bring souls into the kingdom of God and strengthen local churches and believers.

   We have done a lot of ministry in Brazil over the years. During one particular week of ministry, I was assigned an interpreter whose knowledge of English was very limited. I began to worry. *If we can hardly understand each other, how will I be able to speak to other Brazilians in a way they can understand?*

   I would soon find out. We were scheduled to speak in a home packed full of friends and neighbors. I spoke as slowly and deliberately as possible so I would not confuse my new interpreter. However, after several attempts to translate what I was saying into Portuguese, my interpreter looked bewildered. I pressed on, trying to get across to these dear people what Jesus Christ had done for them on the cross. As far as I could tell, all they were getting was a combination of confusing words and even more confusing looks. It was at that moment that I bowed my head and prayed, "Lord, I have come all this way to tell these people of Your love for them. To tell them that their sin can be forgiven through Your Son, Jesus Christ. To give to them a message of hope and life. But I just cannot seem to get through."

When I finished my brief prayer, I looked up and directly into the eyes of a young mother who sat across the room from me. Tears were streaming down her face. It was at that moment that I realized something very important. I felt that I had been a complete failure at communicating the love of God to these dear people. However, God was communicating His love to their hearts in ways I could not see. Before long, this young mother, her husband, and several others in that home received Jesus Christ as their Savior and Lord. I could almost hear Him say to me, "No, Rick, you are not getting through very well, but I am getting through just fine." Through our simple attempts, even when we feel like we are not getting through, God is working!

7. A short-term mission trip may lead to a long-term commitment to a country or people group for years to come. The mission you participate in may be the means by which God launches a mighty work that reaches an untold number of souls for Jesus Christ. It is even possible to adopt an entire people group and begin a focus to plant churches and present a gospel witness among them.

The church that I pastored many years ago has been effective in establishing a Christian witness among the Mina people group of India. The Mina consists of about four and a half million previously unreached souls. In recent years, churches have been planted, and people are beginning to put their faith in Jesus Christ. There is no limit to the impact and influence that a mission team can have on a portion of the world when they commit to a long-term investment.

8. The Lord is at work among the nations. He does not need us, but He invites us to be a part of His story.

Most of us are familiar with John 3:16. However, often we tend to miss the significance of what follows. Go back and read John 3:16-17. Notice how many times the "world" is mentioned. "For God so loved the **world** . . . For God did not send His Son into the **world** to condemn the **world**, but that the **world** through Him might be saved." When God repeats something that many times, it should capture our attention. The point is this: God has the world on His heart. Not just our small part of it, but the whole world is on His heart. If we are going to be faithful followers of our Savior, then we must have His concerns on our hearts as well. Do you have God's heart for the nations?

Scripture teaches that to whom much is given much is required. Since the Great Commission is our mandate from Christ, it should be our desire to use our resources (time, money, prayer, gifts, and abilities) to make disciples of all nations (Matthew 28:19-20). Every Christian and every local church is called to either be a goer or a sender. "How shall they hear without a preacher? And how shall they preach unless they are sent?" (Romans 10:14-15) The impact of short-term missions is endless. The impact it will have on your church and the role it will play in the missional mindset of your people should not be underestimated. God uses missions to change lives, not just the lives of those being reached, but also the lives of those being sent. Have we become gospel hoarders, or are we being good stewards of the resources God has given us? Short-term missions plays a crucial role in how we are giving the gospel to a world in need of hope.

Chapter Two
Answering Common Objections

> *"People who do not know the Lord ask why in the world we waste our lives as missionaries. They forget that they too are expending their lives. And when the bubble has burst, they will have nothing of eternal significance to show for the years they have wasted."*
>
> ~ Nate Saint

In the past fifteen years, I have heard a multitude of doubts and excuses about being involved in short-term missions. Most of these objections fall under a few repeated thoughts and concerns. Perhaps you have had some concerns of your own. Take a look at these common objections and the answers found in God's Word.

Objection 1: Missions should begin at home. We have enough work to do here.

I cannot tell you how many times well-intentioned believers have said this to me. There is no doubt that our mission does begin at home. Acts 1:8 says, "But you will receive power when the Holy Spirit comes on you; and you will be my witnesses in Jerusalem, and in all Judea and Samaria, and to the ends of the earth." As believers who confess Jesus as Lord, our mission begins in our own Jerusalem. It begins in our homes, schools, neighborhoods, businesses, and communities. It would be a great dishonor to our Lord and disobedience to His gospel to ignore all the people around us who have not met our Lord Jesus. Every day, our church members ought to be living out the gospel in their own lives to touch the hearts of those who are closest to them. After all, I did not coin the phrase, "We want to take the gospel across the street and across the globe."

Yes, missions does begin at home, but it cannot stay there or end there. The truth is that there is more mission involvement here in our own Jerusalem than anywhere else in the world. Consider the following statistics about the access we readily have to the gospel.

- There are currently three hundred thousand evangelical churches in the US led by six hundred thousand pastors and church staff (not including independent churches).[1]
- The average American family owns four Bibles.[2]
- The annual expenditure for Bibles in America is $425 million.[3]
- There are 260 theological seminaries in the US that represent over eighty thousand students.[4]
- The American evangelical church operates on more than $15 billion each year. A mere 2 percent of that goes directly toward international missions.[5]

Yes, living for the Great Commission does begin at home. We are pouring our resources into reaching our Jerusalem with the gospel, but have not ventured out to our Judea, Samaria, and the ends of the earth with the same involvement or urgency. If we truly grasped God's heart for the nations, then we would not make excuses to stay here. We cannot afford to be gospel hoarders.

Objection 2: Why spend all that money to go on a trip? It would be better to send the money directly to the missionaries.

There is no doubt that short-term mission trips are expensive. There is also no doubt that missionaries and organizations need more in the way of finances. In recent years, many mission organizations have had to delay mobilizing new missionaries because of a lack of funds.

But money alone is not the answer to successful world missions and evangelism. God uses people. Recently, I had the privilege of preaching in a church located in a small village in the African bush. After the service, I was enjoying a time of fellowship with the pastor and his people. The pastor broke into a wide grin and said, "Thank you for coming. Your coming reminds me that God really does love us." If for no other reason than to encourage this dear pastor who serves the Lord in a difficult area, I would continue to go.

Many people wanted to help Haiti after the earthquake in 2010. Hundreds of organizations and churches rallied to send resources and aid to the Haitian people. However, one of our missionaries recently voiced her concerns about this global effort. She said, "What we needed more during that time was a helping hand. We needed people." Even still, these missionaries are asking us to bring as many teams as we can. They need the church, not just their money.

Yes, short-term trips are costly. However, an expensive trip can be evidence of a fruitful partnership. The missionaries and churches we work with are always in great need. When we take teams to assist and serve alongside them in ministry, we do not want to be a financial burden. I recently heard of a small team that went overseas to help one of our missionaries. They asked this missionary to give them room and board, provide transportation, and organize their ministry activity for the week. At the end of the week the team left and did not compensate the missionary in any way. The missionary was left in a great financial bind and struggled for the next several months to recoup lost money and resources. So please be cautious about "cheap" mission trips.

It is extremely important that we bless our missionaries and care for them. It is my desire to always leave the missionary or church we have worked with in a better financial position than it was when we arrived. Physical efforts partnered with financial help can leave a missionary and church encouraged and strengthened to press on for the gospel another day.

Objection 3: Mission work should be done by those professionally trained or most familiar with the culture they serve.

One of the greatest mission movements in history was led by a group of untrained and uneducated men. In fact, some who observed them even called them ignorant.

> Now when they saw the boldness of Peter and John, and perceived that they were uneducated and untrained men, they marveled. And they realized that they had been with Jesus. (Acts 4:13)

These men had not been educated in a Bible college or seminary. They had never been to a seminar or training session on cross-cultural evangelism. They had simply been with Jesus and captured His desire for all humanity to be saved.

Of course, we should thank God that there are wonderful schools and mission agencies preparing men and women to carry the gospel to foreign lands. Those who have been called to full-time vocational missions should receive as much specialized training as possible. The Lord is using these mission leaders to develop strategies and methods to penetrate many cultures with God's truth. However, we should not be led to believe that only our mission specialists can be used by God to reach people of other cultures, backgrounds, and religions. Anyone who has been transformed by the cross and has experienced the love of Jesus can be an instrument to bring the Word of God to others. The Holy Spirit in us has a way of transcending every barrier and obstacle. I have even seen children become instruments in the hands of God to break through walls of religious and cultural differences.

He uses the trained and untrained, educated and uneducated, young and old, rich and poor. Scripture reminds us of God's plan to use ordinary individuals to accomplish His purposes.

> For you see your calling, brethren, that not many wise according to the flesh, not many mighty, not many noble, *are called*. But God has chosen the foolish things of the world to put to shame the wise, and God has chosen the weak things of the world to put to shame the things which are mighty; and the base things of the world and the things which are despised God has chosen, and the things which are not, to bring to nothing the things that are, that no flesh should glory in His presence. (1 Corinthians 1:26-29)

There are many full-time missionaries who would welcome volunteers to come and assist them in their ministry. Volunteers can help advance the work of a missionary many times over. For example, I heard one of our missionaries say that a mission team has done more work in a week than he could have done in several months by himself

Although formal training is not necessary for a layperson to be involved in a short-term mission trip, churches should still make an effort to prepare their volunteers for the mission. Many concise training opportunities exist to get volunteers ready for mission involvement. We take every one of our volunteers through a training manual specific to the country and culture where we will be ministering.

If we merely wait for the "professionals" to get the message to all nations, the mission will never be completed. Let us join our hearts and hands with them to accomplish this holy task.

Objection 4: There is not proper discipleship or follow-up of new believers from a short-term mission.

A part of any successful strategy in short-term missions should include ongoing discipleship. The Lord has given us His church as the primary tool to accomplish this task. When possible, every volunteer team should be building friendships and partnerships with churches, pastors, and Christian leaders in their country of focus. I have found that there are churches and missionaries in countries outside of the United States that are eager to develop a partnership with volunteer teams. In this way, when the short-term mission is over, workers on-site can conserve the fruit of the mission's labor and continue the mission's work. Rather than taking a "hit or miss" approach to follow-up, the established church or missionary can be ready to begin work when the team has left. The team leader should emphasize the importance of follow-up as a part of their focus and training. One of the great advantages of establishing a partnership with a particular church or organization is the ability to build on the work year after year.

Finally, let us not forget that the blessed Holy Spirit has been following up on new converts for the past two thousand years. He is quite capable of continuing His work in the hearts and lives of those He indwells. In some areas where churches are not yet established, we must trust Him to conserve the work that has been done. When Paul was concerned about the spiritual development of the Philippian believers, he wrote: "being confident of this very thing, that He who has begun a good work in you will complete *it* until the day of Jesus Christ" (Philippians 1:6).

Returning to the same areas was also a part of Paul's strategy. In Acts, we find him making return visits to churches and believers to encourage them and continue to teach them. "Then after some days Paul said to Barnabas, 'Let us now go back and visit our brethren in every city where we have preached the word of the Lord, *and see* how they are doing'" (Acts 15:36). We see the same principle at work in Acts 14.

> And when they had preached the gospel to that city and made many disciples, they returned to Lystra, Iconium, and Antioch, strengthening the souls of the disciples, exhorting *them* to continue in the faith, and *saying*, 'We must through many tribulations enter the kingdom of God.' So when they had appointed elders in every church, and prayed with fasting, they commended them to the Lord in whom they had believed. (Acts 14:21-23)

Your mission team can have an eternal impact on an area by continuing to go there year after year. In this way, the kingdom of God will advance and believers will be encouraged and strengthened.

Objection 5: It is too dangerous to travel overseas.

This is a common objection that I hear all the time. "Are you sure you should be going there? Is it safe? I have heard that there is a lot of trouble over there. It is too risky!" God has called us to take the gospel to all people groups, lands, cultures, and nations. He did not exclude from the Great Commission areas that may be considered dangerous. Now having said that, I do not believe that we should purposefully take a team into an area where volunteers are likely to be injured or even killed. However, the Lord may call specific individuals to go into the risky and extremely dangerous areas. You will need to ask God for great discernment in choosing the location of the mission and the size of the team. For example, a smaller more experienced team of volunteers might be led to a country where it is illegal to preach the gospel. But a team consisting of people of various ages and genders should focus on areas where they can safely travel and minister.

So what about the risks involved in taking a team to another country? There are always risks involved when traveling anywhere. It can be as risky driving across town in Dallas as it is driving across town in Nairobi, Cape Town, San Paolo, or Mumbai. One of the advantages of working with established missionaries or churches in a particular country is that they usually know where a team can go and what areas to avoid.

Take this story, for example. On a recent trip to Port-au-Prince, Haiti, my team of volunteers and I needed to be at a local church across town for a service. The missionary we were helping took us on a longer route than was necessary to avoid an area that was prone to riots. In some countries, local pastors have warned me about areas to stay away from and what times not to be out. The purpose of your mission team is not to encounter as much *danger* as possible, but to minister to people in Jesus' name as *safely* as possible.

Mission volunteers should be given clear instructions on how to avoid dangerous or undesirable situations. This can be done during orientation for the trip and emphasized during each day of the mission. Observing these simple rules will greatly reduce risks regardless of where the team is going.

1. Never go out alone.
2. Travel in groups.
3. Do not go out after dark.
4. Do not talk too loudly.
5. Do not flash money or jewelry around.
6. Avoid areas known for parties, drugs, prostitution, or riots.
7. Do not look like a tourist.

8. Never go out alone.
9. Wear a scowl on your face that says, "Don't even think about messing with me."—Just kidding!
10. Never go out alone.

Most common objections to short-term missions can be summed up in these five areas I've discussed. Regardless, all things considered, I believe in short-term missions. I believe it can change the way we share the gospel. I believe it can encourage and equip the national churches as well as the sending churches. I believe God uses short-term missions to reach a lost world with the news of His redeeming love.

Chapter Three
Choosing Your Mission

"The mission of the church is missions and the mission of missions is the church."
~ Unknown

Once your church makes the decision to undertake a short-term mission project, its leadership should investigate where to go and with whom to work. You will need to answer the following questions as you prepare for your mission.

What country are you being led to focus on year after year? The earthquake that hit Haiti in 2010 has had a profound impact on the spiritual condition of people living in Port-au-Prince. A missionary friend of mine told me, "Never before have we seen the Haitian people so concerned about the things of God than right now. Those who survived the earthquake are asking, 'Why didn't I die? God surely must have a purpose for my life.'" In fact, a recent article about Haiti stated, "A movement of God has swept the tiny island."[6] Some have estimated that nearly two hundred thousand Haitians have come to faith in Jesus, and hundreds of new churches have been planted since the earthquake. In this critical time with so many new believers and new churches, we cannot allow believers in Haiti to stand alone. They need the global church to stand with them.

This increase of faith and planting of churches is happening all over the world. God is working and He is inviting us to be a part of His work. When you get ready for your first short-term mission, find a country like Haiti where God is working and where the church is greatly needed. Allow the Lord to lead you. Ask your church to see His guidance and ask Him to put a particular group of people in your hearts. Then commit to investing into that country long-term. I cannot stress enough the importance of *reentry*. In order for short-term missions to be fully effective, your church must have an ongoing investment in a particular area or nation. You will build lasting relationships with churches, missionaries, pastors, and lay people from that group or country, and they will need your prayer, encouragement, support, and help as often as you can give it. The trip itself may be short, but the impact of a long-term commitment is endless.

What missionary, church, or mission organization do you plan to partner with? It can be extremely dangerous to travel to a strange country unannounced with no plan. You must have a church, missionary, or organization partnering with you and ready for your team when you arrive. There are many good and godly mission organizations making a great impact for the Kingdom of God. Some of them are independent organizations while others are linked to a particular church or denomination. The Southern Baptist Convention, for example, has over five thousand missionaries placed all around the globe.[7] In addition, many missionaries have written specific requests for groups of volunteers to come and help with a project.

In 1996, I took a small volunteer team to Uganda, Africa. There, we worked with a Baptist missionary who was nearing retirement.

We had a wonderful week of sharing the gospel in remote villages and conducting a training conference for dozens of local pastors. During that week I met a young national named Godfrey who was assisting our missionary in ministry. We quickly became friends and enjoyed getting to know each other. That friendship later developed into a ministry partnership that has enabled us to take hundreds of volunteers to Uganda. In the years that followed that first simple mission, we have presented the gospel to tens of thousands of people, seen over twenty thousand come to faith in Jesus, planted eighteen new churches, trained hundreds of pastors, and treated thousands of people in free medical clinics. All of this developed out of a two-week mission trip with a small team of six volunteers.

The possibilities that may develop from your involvement on a mission project are limitless. In Revelation, the Lord Jesus was speaking to the church at Philadelphia when He said, "I know your works. See, I have set before you an open door, and no one can shut it; for you have a little strength, have kept My word, and have not denied My name" (Revelation 3:8). What open door is the Lord placing before you? Will you be obedient and walk through while it is still open? Remember, it may not remain open for long, so go while you still can, but do not go alone. Go alongside someone who knows the country, the people, and the culture.

What type of ministry do you want to be involved in? Part of connecting with a missionary or church on the ground is planning the ministry activity. To do this, recognize a need and meet it head-on. You will need to work closely with your contact to plan and organize details. Remember to be flexible with the one or the ones with whom you are working. Because they know the culture, they will know what boundaries and obstacles you will face in trying to accomplish a particular type of ministry. The following list is not exhaustive, but it includes some of the most common ministry activities available for a mission team.

Construction. You could build homes in Haiti for the millions living in tents or build structures in Uganda for churches meeting under trees. This is a great way to put to use the abilities and talents of men in your church and open doors for the gospel as you work.

Medical. With a medical team you can conduct free clinics in third world countries where the people have little or no access to medical treatment. This is a great way to do one-on-one evangelism with each patient.

VBS. Vacation Bible schools are a great way to share the love of Jesus with the children of a local village or a part of an inner city alike. The word will spread like wildfire, and many children may walk miles to attend. If the children bring their parents with them, you have a great opportunity to reach them as well.

School assemblies. Schools in foreign countries are almost always honored and eager to have students from America come into their classes and speak to their students. Time in the school could include sharing a testimony, playing music, performing a drama, showing a Christian film, presenting the gospel, and allowing time for questions. In most cases, the students will be open and responsive to everything the team has to say.

Prison ministry. Many foreign prisons are in worse conditions than you could imagine. Some of them do not provide the inmates with soap for bathing and do not provide any type of medical care. Inmates receive very little food and almost never have a bed or mat to sleep on. Nevertheless, the inmates and guards will usually welcome your team as honored guests. You will want to schedule the visit long before you arrive and make arrangements to speak with the inmates. This is another great opportunity for the men on your team to minister. You could bring boxes of soap to give out and spend time one-on-one with the inmates before presenting the gospel to everyone. We have seen many inmates as well as guards come to faith in Jesus in this way.

Pastors training. As far as short-term missions is concerned, I do not know of a better way to leave a lasting impact for the gospel than by pouring help into the pastors and church leaders of the nations and groups of people we're trying to help. These are the men who are truly reaching their communities. These pastors know their people and their culture, and have a heart and passion to reach them for Christ. However, the overwhelming majority of them have had little to no biblical education. In fact, the average pastor in Uganda has the equivalent of a sixth grade education. More than that, many third world pastors do not even have a complete copy of God's Word. We have seen some pastors in remote villages share a Bible among each other by tearing out books of and taking turns preaching with them. And yet God is using these men to impact their countries and groups in ways we never could on a two-week trip.

This is why training pastors and church leaders is a great way to truly multiply the work of the gospel. These pastors are starving for someone to teach them. Their teaching should include such things as key biblical doctrines, practical leadership principles, how to prepare a sermon, how to raise up leaders in the church, and other tasks related to serving a church. There is no shortage of biblical teaching that these men desire and desperately need. What you will not have to teach them is how to have a passion for the gospel and a heart for the lost!

One-on-one evangelism. We have been taking mission teams all over the world for nearly two decades. In that time, God has given me the great honor of taking His gospel to over forty different countries (I am praying for fifty by 2015). In all of the opportunities God has given me, I have found that nothing impacts a lost soul more than a one-on-one personal connection. The individual who may quickly turn away from someone preaching to a large crowd will often easily engage a Christian in a personal discussion, especially in foreign lands. I do not want to pretend that cross-cultural evangelism strategies are simple. This kind of evangelism is indeed very complex, and many brilliant men and women have spent a lot of time developing approaches that work. However, it is easy to allow complex mission strategies to overshadow the power of the Holy Spirit through a believer's personal testimony.

Several years ago, one of our volunteer team members was sharing the gospel with a man in Brazil. A local church had been trying to reach this man and his family for a long time with no response. But when the mission volunteer spoke from his heart about the love and grace of God, tears began to form in the eyes of this stubborn Brazilian. He said, "If you would come all the way from America to bring me this message, then I know it must be important. Please tell me more." A few minutes, a simple testimony, and a clear gospel message is all it took for this man to place his faith and trust in Jesus Christ for salvation.

In 2004, two of my sons spent the summer living with my friend Godfrey in Uganda. One day they were at a local coffee shop in downtown Jinja (the second largest town in the country) when a teenage boy approached them and asked why they were there. My sons bought the young man a cup of coffee, sat down at a table, and spent the next several hours talking with him. His name was Ishmael, and his family was the most predominant Muslim family in town.

Ishmael told my sons about how something had been speaking to his heart for several months. "I began having great doubt about my religion and decided to read the Bible," he explained. He said that he had so many questions about Jesus and the Bible that he actually prayed to God and asked Him to send someone who could explain it all to him. He said, "As soon as I saw that you were Americans, I knew I had to speak with you."

And so my sons faithfully took the opportunity God had placed before them to explain the gospel message to this young man. It has been nearly ten years since Ishmael was saved and changed his name to Emmanuel. He underwent great persecution from his family and his community for converting to Christianity. But as a result, nearly his entire family has come to faith in Jesus. We are still praying for Emmanuel's father to be saved.

The point is that God uses His people. We can come up with the most complex and formulated mission strategies known to man, but without the work of the Holy Spirit in the lives of His saints, people will not hear the gospel. One-on-one evangelism is an incredibly effective way to reach the lost. Make sure that it is a part of every mission you take.

It would be very easy to travel to Africa, help build an orphanage, go on a safari, and travel back home without ever sharing the gospel with a single person. That is not a mission. That is a humanitarian trip at best, and tourism at worst. We are doing a great disservice to people and being disobedient to God if we care for the physical needs of someone but do not share with him or her the saving love of God. We must be faithful to give the gospel and not hoard it.

As you pray and prepare for your next mission, examine your ministry. Ask tough questions. Why are we doing this? How does this help further the Kingdom of God? How does this help encourage the church and spread the gospel? In recent years, in this social media era, it has become increasingly popular to be directly involved in trying to change the world. Short-term missions have become very popular. Most of us have the T-shirt, the bracelet, the sticker on our car, or the coffee mug that tells everyone which clean water project we are a part of or which third world orphanage we are supporting.

Choosing Your Mission

You cannot read the newspaper or your Facebook news feed without hearing about someone doing something somewhere in the world for the "greater good." Maybe it is a day going without shoes to raise money for people who don't have shoes, or giving up your two mochas a month for projects in Africa. I am sure it does not hurt that numerous celebrities in film, music, and sports are now becoming prominent advocates of many social concerns including poverty, hunger, orphans, gang violence, HIV/AIDS, slavery, sex trafficking, and clean water. Philanthropy is on the rise!

Is being concerned about these issues a bad thing? Of course not. There is a lot of social injustice out there, and that is putting it lightly. We live in a very sinful, fallen, broken world. As followers of Christ, we are called to serve, to love, and to do good. "If anyone, then, knows the good they ought to do and does not do it, it is sin for them" (James 4:17).

But at the heart of it all, what is our motivation? With the exponential growth of nonprofits in our culture and our direct access to global issues via the Internet and other media, one cannot help but ask the question, is our involvement in the world's issues just trendiness disguised as compassion? And if it is true compassion, then to what end? Are we simply meeting someone's temporary physical needs, or is there a deeper reason? Is our end goal truly to make Christ known to every nation (Matthew 28:16-20)? Is our sole motivation truly to see people come to know Him? It is easy to say that this is our desire, but do we reflect that desire? Do our churches reflect it? Do our short-term mission trips reflect it? My prayer is that in everything we do, everywhere we go, and every trip we take, the gospel will be central. As we install clean water wells, build new orphanages, conduct medical clinics, train young pastors, plant new churches, and make disciples all over the world, may the gospel be at the center of it all, and not a small part of what we do.

Chapter Four
Forming Your Team

"Spirit of Christ is the Spirit of missions, and the nearer we get to Him the more intensely missionary we must become."
~ Henry Martyn

First Corinthians 12 describes the church as the body of Christ with many different members. Each member of the body has a specific function and operation. Your church is also made up of people who have a wide range of spiritual gifts and God-given abilities. Those gifts and abilities can be exercised greatly on a short-term mission team to meet needs, bless lives, and advance the Kingdom of God in this world. Over the years I have had the opportunity to be a part of countless foreign mission teams, and I have always been amazed at the differences between each team member. Every person has something unique to bring to the mission experience.

Several years ago, I took a team to participate in an evangelistic mission in East Africa. When we visited a remote village in the African bush, our purpose was to take the gospel message from house to house (what we like to call "hut-to-hut evangelism"). As usual, we had to speak through the aid of a local interpreter who knew the local language. However, a man from another African country was visiting the village that day and did not speak English or the local language. While trying to find a way to communicate with him, we discovered that he spoke French. To our surprise, a young lady on our team said she had taken years of French in high school and college. She was able to carry on a fluent conversation with him. Even better, she was able to share the love and grace of Jesus with him. As a result of our team member's obedience to share the gospel, this man placed his faith and trust in Christ that day. It was exciting to see how God had placed that young lady on our team with an ability that no one else had. She was able to use that gift to give the message of eternal life to a man from an entirely different country. What a divine appointment!

You may find that members of your team possess a variety of gifts and abilities. It may be that God will meet a special need that no one else can meet through someone on your team. However, it is important that the type of ministry you plan should match the type of team you have assembled. For example, you would not want to plan a medical mission but then only take a team of construction men. It is crucial that the team you have assembled matches the mission your have chosen. Ideally the Lord is leading you and your church to invest in a particular area long-term. We have a church that partners with us in Uganda each year. They are taking two to three trips a year, and each one is different. One trip might be for pastors training, while another one is specifically a medical mission. They assemble their teams based on the type of ministry the church will be a part of on that particular trip. This church is deeply invested in the people of Uganda, and they are building lasting relationships there with the churches, pastors, and villages with whom they are working. Their work is a great example of how to do short-term missions well.

There are also other things to consider when forming your team. Over the years, I have worked with hundreds of volunteers serving on mission teams. I believe that most of these individuals were a blessing to those to whom they ministered. However, there have been a few individuals who were not spiritually mature enough to be involved. Their immaturity created difficulty for our team and the nationals we were trying to reach. Having said that, let us look at some of the qualifications a volunteer should have in order to participate on a team. The following questions will help you discern whether a person is a good candidate for a short-term mission.

1. **Does the volunteer demonstrate a real and vital relationship with Jesus Christ?** It is difficult for a volunteer to share something with others that is not real in his or her own life. Every person participating on the team should be able to give a clear testimony about his or her salvation and what it means to be a follower of Jesus. Uncertainty about this most important relationship will be a setback on any mission. If the person has difficulty expressing their testimony, ask them to write it down. Some people express themselves more clearly in writing. The important thing for a mission leader to be certain of is that each person has had a personal salvation experience with Jesus Christ.

2. **Does the volunteer exhibit a growing relationship with Jesus Christ?** It is unfortunate that a large number of believers have stopped growing in their relationship with Christ. They often see their life with Christ as "business as usual" and have no real discipleship or mentoring in their lives. The spiritual nature of our mission *demands* that we be committed followers of Jesus Christ, and

radically obedient to the Great Commission. A half-hearted disciple will only produce other half-hearted disciples. That kind of Christ-follower will never change the world.

3. **Is the volunteer involved in a local church?** I have talked with a number of people who expressed interest in going on a mission trip who were not involved in a local church. They were either church-hoppers, inconsistent in their church involvement, or not connected with any church at all. It is difficult to express the importance of the local church to new believers on a mission trip when our own volunteers do not understand the importance of one. We want to work through and connect people with established national churches when at all possible. The church is the bride of Christ and is the instrument He uses in bringing the gospel to a lost world. We should love and be committed to His church. "Christ loved the church and gave himself up for her to make her holy, cleansing her by the washing with water through the word, and to present her to himself as a radiant church, without stain or wrinkle or any other blemish, but holy and blameless" (Ephesians 5:25-27).

4. **Does the volunteer exhibit a servant's attitude?** The focus of any mission—whether medical, construction, orphan care, teaching, or another ministry—is to serve. We are called to serve others, putting our own needs and comforts aside. On one of our first trips we took overseas years ago, we had a team member who did not reflect the heart of a servant. We were eating in a local restaurant in a third world country when this individual began to

gripe and complain about not having ice in her drink. She proceeded to create a big commotion and drew the attention of all of the nationals around her. She called over our waitress and demanded to have ice. The situation was resolved quickly, but not until after the damage had been done. On the mission field (or anywhere in life), there can be no room for self-centeredness, arrogance, or pride.

5. **Will the volunteer respect authority?** The very nature of international travel makes it extremely important to follow instructions and respect authority. When team members have their own agendas or believe that they are not beholden to obey guidelines, rules, and laws, they create problems for the entire team. This kind of disobedience can cause complications with airport security, the local government, or the national churches or missionaries where you are working. International travel can also be dangerous if members of your team do not follow clear instructions. Each team member should display a clear willingness to submit to authority.

6. **Will the volunteer work for team unity?** Division and disunity on a team hinders the effectiveness of the mission. It also gives a poor testimony about the volunteers and the churches they represent. We are reminded to strive and work for the unity of all believers in Ephesians 4.

> As a prisoner for the Lord, then, I urge you to live a life worthy of the calling you have received. Be completely humble and gentle; be patient, bearing with one another in love. Make every effort to keep the unity of the Spirit through the bond

of peace. There is one body and one Spirit, just as you were called to one hope when you were called; one Lord, one faith, one baptism; one God and Father of all, who is over all and through all and in all. (Ephesians 4:1-6)

On one of our teams several years ago, we had two men who differed on a particular point of theology. For the duration of our mission they bickered and argued with each other without any consideration of who was watching or listening. Years later, we were back in that same county when one of our interpreters asked about those two American men who could never get along with each other. He said, "That was very sad. Those two men never seemed to stop arguing." This interpreter never forgot those men. We may never know the full extent of the damage that is caused when there is division between believers. A team united by the strong bonds of our Lord Jesus Christ speaks volumes to those who are being served. They will know we are followers of Jesus Christ by our love, cooperation, and unity in the Spirit.

7. **Is the volunteer free of habits and vices that could hinder the effectiveness of the team?** This is not an attempt to be demanding or legalistic. It is a reminder that certain habits and behaviors can be offensive in other cultures and to the very people we are seeking to reach with the gospel. It should be understood that the use of tobacco products, alcohol, or profanity could destroy the work of the mission. In many cultures, these things are seen as signs of rebellion or wickedness and are not associated with God's people. Those who struggle with such things should be encouraged to wait until they have

mastered these habits by the power of the Holy Spirit. Then they will be free of anything that might hinder their gospel witness. I have had the opportunity to lead people on mission trips who were at many different stages of spiritual growth. We want to involve volunteers who are growing in their faith and Christlikeness.

8. **Does the volunteer have physical or emotional challenges that need to be considered?** The age of a volunteer does not disqualify them from a mission team. I have served alongside people in their eighties who were wonderfully used of the Lord. However, the age and physical ability of a volunteer should be matched with the kind of mission in which they participate. I would not take an elderly team member on a trip that requires a great amount of physical exertion. Carefully consider the emotional stability of the volunteer as well. The great poverty, disease, and hardship encountered on one of our recent trips proved to be too much for one of our team members. This individual became very depressed and lethargic and was unable to continue with the mission. Travel and ministry in third world countries may be too emotionally demanding for some people. This is another reason why a simple training or orientation meeting is important as you prepare your team.

Remember, though, that the purpose of examining each mission volunteer is not to build an exclusive group of the best and brightest missionaries. Obedience to the Great Commission is not a calling for the few or the most qualified. It is the calling for every follower of Jesus Christ. However, these examinations are the means of helping each person determine his or her readiness for a foreign mission.

Those who are not yet ready can be challenged to continue to grow in the grace and knowledge of our Lord Jesus Christ. In time, with appropriate discipleship and training, they may make the very best servants on the mission field.

Chapter Five
Sharing the Gospel Cross-Culturally

"Living obediently in God's call to go wherever and do whatever to make Him known—that is the heart beat of every missionary."
~ Kevin Ezell

The very nature of the word *gospel* implies that we have a glorious and wonderful message to proclaim. It is unfortunate that there are many believers who do not grasp how to clearly and simply present this good news—this message of salvation.

When the angel announced the birth of the Messiah to the shepherds, he said, "Do not be afraid, for behold, I bring you good tidings of great joy which will be to all people" (Luke 2:10). There are two outstanding thoughts that appear in this powerful verse of scripture. First, the angel announced that the message was full of good news. In other words, *the gospel*. Try reading it this way: "I bring you *the gospel* which will be to all people." Pretty incredible. Of course, we understand that the angel is speaking about Jesus. He will bring true joy to all those who receive Him. Second, this good news was not just for a select group of people. The angel proclaimed that it is for "all people." Every race, group, economic status, skin color, and social ranking can be made right before God through of His Son Jesus.

God has given us the opportunity and privilege to proclaim the gospel to anyone who will listen. I have found that people from other countries and cultures are eager to hear the message about God's love and forgiveness. In fact, it may prove to be more difficult to present this message in our own culture than in many other parts of the world—however, I have been in some Muslim countries that are the exception to this statement. Yet, even in some difficult, hostile countries, I have found that people are generally open to discuss their personal views about the Christian faith in general and Jesus Christ in particular.

I consistently remind those who are going on a mission trip that the primary purpose is to present the gospel to those we meet. When conducting a medical clinic, we want our patients to know that we are bringing them something far more important than simply medicine and treatment. The medicine will only last for a brief time at best. The gospel we bring will last through eternity. It is well and good to do good in as many ways as we can, whether through food distribution, medical assistance, providing personal provisions, or any other kind of aid. However, we have not done anyone eternal good until we have offered them the opportunity to hear about God's provision of salvation from our sin through the Lord Jesus Christ.

It is certainly true that it is easier to share about our faith in Jesus in some places than in others. In East Africa, we are able to talk freely about our faith. Yet, in some Asian and Middle-Eastern countries, we have to be much more discreet in how we introduce the subject. Studying the spiritual climate of an area will help you better prepare for the mission. We will discuss various situations that you can encounter while on a mission in the next chapter. For now, let us focus on the major factors in sharing the gospel in a foreign land.

The gospel is all about Jesus Christ. When presenting our witness or personal testimony, the focus must always be on Him. Focus on His purpose for coming into the world (to deal with sin), His divine nature as the Son of God, His death on the cross as the payment for our sin, and His glorious resurrection. These are key elements of any gospel presentation. There are many tried and proven methods of sharing the gospel. I am not concerned that everyone uses the same approach or strategy. I am concerned that each person is able to verbalize his or her faith in Jesus freely and easily. Like anything else we do, each person will get better as they practice sharing the message. Do not feel like you need to reinvent the wheel every time. Find a method that you feel most comfortable with and master it.

Here are a few examples of effective gospel presentations:

- *Steps to Peace with God* by the Billy Graham Evangelistic Association
- *Four Spiritual Laws* by Campus Crusade for Christ
- *Evangelism Explosion* by Coral Ridge Presbyterian Church
- *FAITH* by the Southern Baptist Convention
- *The Story* by SpreadTruth

These are just a few of the organizations that have produced excellent materials to help prepare your team to share the gospel with everyone they meet. If we do not find a way in which to effectively communicate the message of Jesus Christ while on a mission for him, we are doing nothing more than the Red Cross or any other humanitarian organization. We are not the Red Cross. However, we are a group of individuals whose lives have been changed by the cross that was stained red by the blood of Jesus Christ. We are not the Peace Corps. However, we are a band of believers who present a message of peace through the One who is called the Prince of Peace.

We are not Lions Club. However, we do talk about the One who is called the Lion of the tribe of Judah. We are not People For the American Way. However, we are ambassadors who represent God's way. We are not Invisible Children. However, we are children of God who want to make visible the only One who can truly save.

I am not in any way making light of the work that many good organizations such as the ones I've named are doing. They have offered life-saving assistance to people all over the world. What I am saying is that *our* mission is to go beyond meeting physical needs alone. We are meeting the spiritual needs of people who, without Christ, have no hope for tomorrow or eternity. Jesus asked, "What will it profit a man if he gains the whole world, and loses his own soul?" (Mark 8:36). What good have we done if we provide people in need with clothing, food, medicine, and clean water, but have not given them the living water of Jesus Christ?

Suggestions to Help in Presenting God's Word

Scripture reminds us that His Word is what this world needs. Jesus said, "Man shall not live by bread alone, but by every word that proceeds from the mouth of God" (Matthew 4:4). The writer of Hebrews said, "For the word of God *is* living and powerful, and sharper than any two-edged sword, piercing even to the division of soul and spirit, and of joints and marrow, and is a discerner of the thoughts and intents of the heart" (Hebrews 4:12). The prophet Isaiah reminds us that God has said, "So shall My word be that goes forth from My mouth; It shall not return to Me void, but it shall accomplish what I please, and it shall prosper *in the thing* for which I sent it" (Isaiah 55:11). When we are armed with these promises, finding ways to get His Word into the hands and hearts of people is exciting.

Bibles. Distributing Bibles and portions of the Scriptures are a great way to share the Word of God. There are Bible societies and other organizations who print Bibles and portions of Scripture in many different languages. On a number of occasions I have had the joy of giving people the very first Bible they have ever owned in their own language. Can you imagine the impact on the lives of your team members when they see someone's eyes light up or tears roll down their cheeks as they hold a copy of God's Word for the very first time? I was on a Bible distribution mission several years ago in a Muslim nation. I tried to give a young man a New Testament, but when he recognized what it was he became angry and refused it. A few minutes later another young man walked by, and I offered him the same New Testament. When he realized what it was, he embraced it and began kissing it. He looked at me with a smile and then looked toward heaven. The last time I saw him, he was clutching his Bible to his heart.

The Gospel of John is a great scripture portion to distribute widely because it is small enough to pack in bundles. On a recent trip to Haiti, we were able to deliver thousands of these Gospel of John booklets in Creole in the city of Port-au-Prince. We literally had people running across the street to get their copy. I always love using John's gospel in an evangelistic outreach like this. John himself tells us the purpose of his writing this gospel in chapter 20. "These are written that you may believe that Jesus is the Christ, the Son of God, and that believing you may have life in His name" (John 20:31). Amen!

Booklets. Gospel tracts and booklets have been used for years to present the gospel because they are saturated with God's Word. I like to take a good supply of tracts and booklets in the language of the nation or people to whom I am ministering. On many occasions, I have had the opportunity to give out a booklet when there was not enough time to talk or no interpreter to help me. I have received several letters and emails over the years from people who received a gospel booklet and later received Jesus as their Savior.

I was speaking at a prison in Cape Town, South Africa several years ago. The prison officials only allowed me a brief time to meet inmates and speak to them. I had some gospel pamphlets that I had written and was able to give them to a number of men as I was leaving the prison. Two months later, I received a letter from one of the prisoners. He wrote to tell me of his trusting in Jesus Christ as a result of reading the booklet I had given him. I was able to keep in touch with him and send him a Bible and other materials to help him grow.

Personal testimony. Your own personal testimony can have a great impact on the lives of others. On a short-term mission where you are constantly meeting people, you will be surprised by how many opportunities you will have to share your testimony in a personal conversation. Perhaps you want to write down your testimony and have it translated into the local language. Several years ago, I was in Ho Chi Minh City, Vietnam. My main objective was to spend a week training pastors who served the underground churches. However, I still wanted a way to discretely give the gospel to Vietnamese people I met during the week. I wrote out my testimony on one side of a sheet of paper and asked my interpreter to translate it on the other side. She was happy to do so. I then had copies made at a local print shop and was able to use that simple sheet of paper to discretely hand out the gospel everywhere I went.

Your testimony does not need to be long. Simply write about the ways that Jesus Christ has worked in your life. It is always best to have someone who knows the language and culture to check it out for anything that could be offensive or misunderstood. I have found this to be extremely helpful when learning how to best communicate the love of Jesus Christ in difficult areas like Vietnam. Be sure to write simply, without phrases that unbelievers may not understand. For example, not everyone will understand the term *saved*, but everyone is aware of a need for forgiveness, comfort, peace, and an assurance of eternal life.

Film. A great tool that has been used to bring the gospel to millions of people is *The Jesus Film* produced by Campus Crusade for Christ. It is available in two hundred languages and can be shown on a projector screen, a computer, or even a mobile device. There are other great films as well that can communicate the gospel across cultural barriers.

Audio. The Bible is available on CD and other audio formats, such as a small portable player called "The Proclaimer" that is made by a ministry called Faith Comes By Hearing. This device can be left with an entire village or community that has no Bible or church.

Apps. Many of the resources I have already mentioned in this chapter are available for download on your mobile device. Technology is an ever-changing, limitless resource that I believe the Christian community has just barely begun to utilize.

There are so many new and exciting ways to help get the Word of God into the hands of people all around the world. When you pray about your next mission, ask God to show you how to best communicate His Word to those you are going to reach. Pray and strategize on ways to meet people and give a witness about Jesus Christ to them. Remember, God loves those people and desires for them to be saved (2 Peter 3:9).

Being Winsome to Win Some

The great apostle Paul was always looking for effective ways to communicate the gospel message. In his first letter to the church at Corinth he said, "I have become all things to all men, that I might by all means win some" (1 Corinthians 19:22). Keeping those words in mind, let us consider some practical ways you can open doors for the gospel on the mission field.

1. Smile. Even when you do not know the language, a simple smile can communicate volumes to another person. Smile sincerely and smile often. The joy of the Lord will always transcend cultural barriers.
2. When beginning a conversation, ask open-ended questions. These can include, "What kind of work do you do?", "Are you in school?", "What are you studying?", "Have you had the opportunity to travel to other places?" Most people enjoy talking about their personal interests, families, school, work, etc. If you find something you both have in common, run with it. Opening the conversation this way tends to calm nerves and make the exchange more natural.
3. Always seek to be positive. Find something to complement about their country, people, or scenery. Avoid getting drawn into discussions about governments, politics, or other divisive social issues.
4. Avoid an egotistical attitude. You may think you can improve many things about their culture and lifestyle. But you are not there to change their government or their cultural habits; you are presenting to them the hope and life found in Jesus Christ.
5. Ask them to teach you some simple words in their language and repeat these words back to them. It almost always gets a laugh.
6. When you feel like the ice has been broken, ask them if you can give them something that is very important in your life. When they give you permission, present them

with the New Testament booklet or other materials in their language. Very seldom have I been refused after beginning a warm and friendly conversation with someone.
7. Be prepared to explain to them the central message of the gospel.
8. Avoid using Christian terminology that they may not understand.
9. Ask them what they think about the message you have shared with them.
10. Be careful not to attack their religious beliefs, place of worship, or doubts about the Christian faith. Keep the conversation focused on Jesus.
11. Help to correct their misconceptions. Always bring them back to Scripture. A simple verse from God's Word has more power and authority than all of our arguments, ideas, and insights combined.
12. Constantly remind yourself that the person you are talking with is someone God loves. Genuine compassion will show through.
13. When your conversation has ended, the individual you are speaking with may or may not be ready to make a decision. Do not force the issue. Ask if you can pray for them. Pray for the Holy Spirit to work deeply in their hearts. Keep them on your prayer list. Remember that God's Word will not return void. Even if the person does not respond positively to the gospel, God is able to use your conversation to reach their hearts down the road. You may be planting a seed for the gospel that someone else will harvest in the future.

14. If the person expresses a desire to enter into a relationship with the Lord Jesus, lead them to make a confession of faith. Explain to them how to express their heart to God. Be patient and clear. You may be speaking with someone who has never prayed or knows little about prayer.
15. If the person places their faith and trust in Jesus Christ for salvation, rejoice with them! Encourage them and if possible leave them with some materials to answer the common question of "Now what do I do?"
16. Whenever possible, get information about the person so that a local church, pastor, or missionary can follow up with the decision they made and begin discipleship.

Speaking through an Interpreter

One of the great challenges for any mission team is the language barrier. Many of us are not fluent in any other language than our own. So how do we communicate the message of the cross with someone who does not speak English? Thankfully, there are people who can help us because they know both languages. We call them interpreters because they take our words and translate them into the native language. Speaking through an interpreter requires patience and practice.

I wish I could say that I have never had any trouble when using an interpreter, but I cannot. Some of my common mistakes have been stumbling on my words, speaking too fast, or using slang terms that get lost in translation. So let me share with you a few simple guidelines I have learned that may help you avoid making the same mistakes.

1. Speak slowly and clearly. When you speak too rapidly or with a heavy accent, your interpreter will have difficulty understanding you.
2. Try to use the simplest words you can. Your interpreter may not be familiar with complex words and expressions.
3. Avoid using slang. Although you may be very comfortable using slang expressions, the chances are your interpreter will have no idea what you are trying to say. I had a friend who was speaking to a group of people in an Asian country. He was extremely excited about being able to share his testimony. The first words out of his mouth were, "Well, I'm just tickled pink to be here." Can you imagine the difficulty the interpreter had with that one?
4. Use short statements. Your interpreter will be able to remember a brief sentence better than a long paragraph. Give your interpreter time to catch up before you begin speaking again.
5. Look directly at the individual or audience with whom you are speaking. You want to engage them, not stare at your interpreter.
6. Remember to speak directly to the individual or audience. This will allow your interpreter to translate your words more naturally. Avoid giving your interpreter orders, which includes statements like, "Tell him that I said he must..."
7. Be patient with your interpreter. It can be very difficult to remember two languages at the same time and switch back and forth between them.

8. Build a relationship with your interpreter. The better he or she gets to know you, the easier it will be for them to translate for you.
9. Find out if your interpreter knows the Lord. Remember the story of Ishmael and my two sons from chapter three? He was saved as a result of interpreting the gospel message over and over for my son.
10. To prevent embarrassing miscommunication, rely on your interpreter to help you avoid statements that may be offensive in his or her culture. While sharing a personal testimony, for example, one of my pastor friends referred to his dating life before he met his wife. However, the culture he was visiting considered dating to involve acts of immorality.

Sharing the gospel cross-culturally can be very challenging. However, if we are truly acting and speaking from the Holy Spirit in us, we can always trust Him with the results. Sometimes He allows us to see the harvest, and sometimes we are the ones planting the seed.

One year we were conducting a free medical clinic in a poor village in East Africa. When people learned that we were there, they walked for miles from every direction to reach us. One of the many hundreds of Africans who came was Mohammed. He was head and shoulders taller than anyone else in the village. I also noticed that his face seemed hard and stone-like. I never saw him smile or change his demeanor the entire day. I knew by his name that he was either a Muslim or had been raised in a Muslim family. I soon found out that he was both.

When I first spoke with Mohammed, he seemed very argumentative. I told him that we were Christians and we had come to the village to give medical and spiritual help for his people. I told him that the medicine would bring healing for their bodies, but only Jesus Christ would bring healing for their souls. He did not agree. We entered into a discussion about who Jesus Christ is and why He came to earth. Mohammed argued that Jesus was only a prophet and not the Son of God. He further asserted that Jesus Christ had not died on the cross for our sins and could not offer salvation.

Throughout the day, we spoke about the sacrifice of Jesus on the cross, His claim to be God in the flesh, and the need to receive Him as Savior and Lord. Several times throughout the day I showed Mohammed verses from the Bible (John 14:6; John 3:16; Isaiah 53:5-6). After each encounter, Mohammed would become angry and walk away. He would walk around the clinic area watching our team at work. Sometimes I would see him glaring in my direction, and before long he was back for another round of debate.

This went on for two full days. On the third and final day of our clinic, I spotted Mohammed in the crowd. This time, the look on his face was not harsh, but one of worry and concern. As he walked in my direction, I saw him carrying a little child. It was his daughter, and she was hot with fever as a result of malaria.

When Mohammed approached me he said, "Please, can you get some help for my daughter? She became sick in the night." I took his daughter from his arms and took her into the medical clinic.

Sometime later, I came out of the clinic carrying his daughter. She had been treated for malaria and given medicine to take for the rest of the week. I explained to Mohammed the dosage of the medicine she would need and then placed her back in his arms. His stony face seemed to melt before me. There was no debating and no arguing. He looked at me with a slight smile and said, "Thank you for helping my daughter."

I told him that I would be praying for him as I traveled back to America, and that I believed that one day he would see that Jesus

Christ truly is the Son of God who died for his sins. I shared with him that I believed he would one day experience God's love and forgiveness in his life.

"Maybe so," he said with a smile, and we parted ways.

All through the following year, I prayed for him. I asked God to reveal Himself to Mohammed and show him that the Lord Jesus is the way, the truth, and the life—the only way of salvation. The next year we returned to East Africa with our mission team. Once again, we went to the same remote village where I had met Mohammed the year before. When we arrived, several hundred Africans greeted us with waving and cheering. I looked over the crowd of people as many pressed in close to shake my hand and greet me. Then I spotted a man who was head and shoulders taller than all the rest. This man resembled Mohammed in certain ways, only he was beaming with joy.

That could not be Mohammed, could it? I thought. But the longer I looked at him, the more familiar he looked. I made my way toward him and we met in the midst of a sea of people.

"Mohammed?" I asked.

"Yes, it is me!" he said with his bright African teeth shining through his smile.

I did not really need to ask the question; his face was beaming with the answer. But I asked him, anyway. "Mohammed, have you received Jesus Christ as your Savior and Lord?"

A wider grin broke upon his face as he said, "Yes, I have. I am now following Jesus Christ." The expression on his face told me that what he was saying was true.

We will never know all that God is doing in the hearts of people. You may share the gospel with hundreds and never see one person come to faith in Christ. But do not be discouraged, because the Holy Spirit is working. He was working long before we arrived, and He will be working there long after we are gone. We have been given a mandate, a mission, to spread the message of God's saving love and grace to a world that desperately needs Him. Be faithful to that task and trust the Lord with the rest.

CHAPTER SIX
Managing Logistics

> *"Some of us are senders & some are goers. Neither is more important than the other. Neither is possible without the other."*
> ~ DAVID SILLS

Taking on a short-term mission project is a massive task. There are numerous administrative hurdles and a thousand details to organize and manage. So, let me commend you for following the Lord in obedience to this mission. This is where the rubber meets the road. We can talk all day about the strategies and methodologies of missions, but this is where we actually have to put feet to it. This is where careful planning, a lot of prayer, and the Holy Spirit have to come in to the equation. Let me walk you through some important steps to take in order to have a productive and safe short-term mission trip.

Confirm the Dates. Contacting the missionary or the church you want to partner with should always be a first step. You do not want to begin promoting a particular date for your trip until you have first confirmed that date with your contact in the country. Several factors go into choosing dates for your trip. First, ask yourself what will work best for the missionary or the church you want to serve. You want to be the most help to them as possible, so find a time when they are in most need of help. Second, the type of team you want to take is also a determining factor. A team of students will most likely have to travel during the summer or during a semester break. Third, the type of ministry you want to be involved in can help determine what time of year you go. For example, the temperature stays well over one hundred degrees in the summer months in Haiti. This would not be the best time to do construction ministry.

Determine the Ministry. After you confirm the dates, work with the missionary or church to determine the ministry activities in which you will be involved. Learn about their work and do what will help them most. For example, if your missionary's work focuses primarily on equipping pastors and encouraging churches, then construct your ministry around these needs. You do not want to try to start something that will hinder the missionary's current focus. Remember, they have strategies in place to reach their people, and you are there to bless and help them, not to make them accommodate your agenda. Refer to chapter three for possible ministry activities.

Develop the Budget. Next, you will need to work with your missionary or church to develop a budget for your trip. The missionary or church can give you estimates for costs in the field, but you will need to estimate all of the other expenses. The following is an example of itemized expenses to be prepared for.

- Lodging
- Food and Water (in transit and in-country)
- Airfare (tickets, taxes, and baggage costs)
- Ground transportation (stateside and on location)
- Visas and other in-country taxes
- Ministry (Bibles, materials, and other special projects)

- Tips (drivers, cooks, housekeepers, etc.)
- Honorariums (for host churches, interpreters, etc.)
- Miscellaneous (be prepared for unforeseen circumstances)

Use your budget to find the total cost of each individual's trip. You will also need to determine how much money you will need to travel with. Can you wire-transfer some of the funds ahead of time? Doing this can be helpful if you are staying with a missionary or church and they need to purchase your food before you come or make other general arrangements. Also ask yourself who will be responsible for the finances. It is always a good idea to travel with an international credit card for emergencies. However, you will use cash to pay for daily expenses such as drivers, food, water, tips, etc. Be prepared to travel with large sums of cash.

Recruit the Team. When you have determined your dates, ministry activity, and total cost for the trip, you are ready to recruit your team. As you do, verify that each member meets the requirements to be involved (see chapter four). Form your team as soon as possible. You will want to give your team members adequate time to raise the needed funds and to fully prepare for the trip. To help your team out, come up with a payment plan so members do not have to pay for their trips in one lump sum. This will also give you the needed funds to begin preparation for the trip (e.g. purchasing airline tickets). Have team members fill out an application and turn it in with a deposit toward their trip. The application should include all basic information, passport information, and spiritual assessment. If you do not know the applicant personally you may want to require a pastoral recommendation. Send the entire team frequent correspondence and updates. This will help keep them informed as well as energized about the trip.

As your departure day approaches, we strongly recommend that you conduct a formal half-day training meeting (or several). This will

Managing Logistics

allow the team to begin building unity as well as give members the opportunity to ask questions. This is your time to fully communicate essential details about travel, ministry, and life in a foreign country. Set aside a special time for prayer as well. Refer to chapter seven for a suggested prayer guide.

Raising Funds

Most of us cannot just write a large check to pay for an expensive mission trip. However, this is where the church comes in! Part of taking the gospel to a world in need of hope is a support team sending us. Paul expressed the importance of senders in Romans 10 when he wrote, "How then shall they call on Him in whom they have not believed? And how shall they believe in Him of whom they have not heard? And how shall they hear without a preacher? And how shall they preach unless they are sent?" (Romans 10:14-15). Raising funds for a mission trip can be exciting as you watch the Lord miraculously provide for your every need. The Holy Spirit can also use this time to grow your faith and trust in Him.

Here are some helpful hints that I believe will make this fundraising experience one that you can look back on and see as a faith-builder.

1. Write a support letter. Your letter should include information about the country and culture, a description of what you will be doing, why you want to be involved in this mission, how you would like the reader to be involved, details about the cost of the trip, and clear instructions on how the reader can give money. Send your letter to family, friends, churches, employers, and businesses. Most people want to help if they cannot go

themselves. Include a self-addressed stamped envelope (SASE) with your support letter.
2. Make arrangements to speak to your church, Sunday school class, or another small group.
3. Begin raising funds as soon as possible. It may take some time for people to respond.
4. Be willing and ready to make sacrifices. Do not expect others to make financial sacrifices that you are not willing to make. You can save money by not eating out, not going on an extravagant vacation, or not buying that new lawn mower. Many people like to put their annual tax return toward their trip. You can also do things like hold a yard sale, sell cupcakes, work overtime, or pick up other side jobs. Save every penny you can and be ready to make sacrifices of your own.

In-Field Logistics

You have confirmed the general information about the trip, but now it is time to really get the ball rolling and nail down specifics. Remain in constant contact with the missionary or church you will be helping and work together to organize details. As the departure day approaches, it is easy to become overwhelmed by all that needs to be done. Create a simple checklist to help you stay on track and not be unprepared.

Ministry itinerary. Showing up in a foreign country without a game plan cannot only put your team in real danger, it can also compromise the success of the mission. You want to be as useful for the Kingdom as you can in such a short period of time, so a clear ministry itinerary is essential. This is not to say that you should not be willing to make changes to the schedule as needed. Anyone who has been overseas knows that flexibility and patience are absolute musts! Things can (and will) change at a moment's notice. As a team leader, you must have the ability to adjust to those changes quickly and efficiently.

Work with your missionary or church and come up with a basic schedule for each day. What time does the team need to be up each morning? What time does the team need to depart for ministry? Will everyone go to the same location, or will you divide the team into sub teams to carry out different tasks? What time does the team need to be back each evening? In many countries being out after dark can be dangerous. Plan your ministry during daylight hours and make the most of it. I also encourage you to schedule a team meeting and devotion time each evening, usually after dinner. This is a great time for your team to share testimonies about the day and ask questions regarding the next day of ministry.

Cultural guidelines. In addition to details about ministry, you need to determine details about living conditions for your team. This requires you to be as knowledgeable as possible about the particular country where you are ministering and living and the culture(s) you will encounter. Are there areas to avoid or situations to be aware of before you get to your destination? Have there been any recent political or governmental issues in the country? Are there currently any travel alerts for Americans? Once, I was on a mission in an Asian country where a hostile demonstration was taking place. Our team quickly found out that the riot was against Americans. We laid low and remained in our hotel for the day. The next day we were able to safely resume our mission without any difficulties. This is an example of why it is always important to stay alert and flexible. You may be required to make last minute adjustments to your schedule for a variety of reasons.

Study the history, the culture(s), important events, places of interest, and the first missionaries in the country or area to which you will be ministering. Also, find out what religious and political obstacles the church there is facing. Be as informed as possible before you go. Doing this research will help you establish clear rules and guidelines for your team. These guidelines should include instructions for appropriate dress and general conduct. In some places, for example, shorts, tank tops, and other clothing that shows skin is a sign of rebellion and can be very offensive. If a team member's clothing causes offense to someone you are ministering to, that may destroy everything you have tried to accomplish.

Also learn about cultural taboos in the area your mission team will serve. In Muslim countries, women are required to wear head coverings when out in public. Also note that certain hand gestures may be harmless to us, but are highly offensive in their culture.

In addition, do not be alarmed when the poor and needy approach you for money or food, but be cautious about handing things out in public. When a sea of people surround you, it will not take long for a riot to erupt. Once when I was in Uganda, one of our team members attempted to give a little boy in a village a piece of candy. Only a few seconds passed before a dozen children saw it and began begging her for a piece. She tried to be generous to each and every child, but before long she had what seemed like hundreds of little Ugandan children swarming her. She threw the bag of candy into the air, which created a roar of excitement. But what seemed like a harmless idea quickly turned out to be very disastrous for the small children who were trampled by the stampede of kids.

Know the culture and prepare your team to be ready for anything. This is for everyone's safety.

Room and Board. Before you go, determine what your accommodations will be. Will you be staying in a hotel, guesthouse, church, mission compound, individual homes, or tents? Where will you be eating your meals? Will there be clean water to drink or will you need to purchase bottled water? Typically, your team will eat breakfast and dinner at the location where you are staying. However, what are the lunch arrangements? You may want to have your team pack a small lunch for each day of ministry. We often encourage our teams to bring something that can be consumed quickly on the go, such as protein bars or crackers. What are the sleeping arrangements? In many cases you may need to provide your own linens, towels, and toiletries.

Transportation. This is often the most overlooked detail in short-term missions. You will most likely not work with a missionary who owns a large van. Many churches do not even have walls, much less a church bus. You will need to arrange for transportation not just to and from the airport, but also to and from the ministry sites each day. Do not just hope to find a taxi when you get there. Taking one can be dangerous and unreliable. On one of our recent trips to Haiti, we met a man who had traveled alone to do some ministry work. He landed in Port-au-Prince and jumped into a random taxi. A few moments later, the taxi driver and an accomplice robbed him at gunpoint, taking his money, belongings, and even his passport. I do not share this story to alarm you, but to urge you to make all of your arrangements beforehand. An impromptu excursion to another country is an easy way to end up in a less than desirable situation.

Make sure you communicate any other needs to your missionary or church beforehand. For example, you will want to arrange to have good interpreters for each day of ministry. Making last minute preparations for ministry in a third world country can sometimes be difficult, so your missionary will need time to pull details together.

Stateside Logistics

Much of the planning that goes into a short-term mission involves your time months in advance and may not necessarily involve your missionary on the ground. Because there are many details to organize and loose ends to tie up, you may want to share the load. Involve your other team members or other leaders within your church. Taking on responsibility can help them take ownership in the mission and increase enthusiasm. Not to mention, it will greatly help you.

Airline tickets. Purchase your airline tickets as soon as you can. You can usually get a cheaper rate when you book in advance. You will need each team member's full name as it appears on his or her passport, his or her date of birth, and passport number. You may also want to go through a travel agent. An established travel agency can help you obtain group tickets or even missionary fare. Group and missionary rates are not only less expensive, but they also usually allow more checked bags. However, as a general rule, a travel agency can save you money when you are traveling from east to west, but not when you are traveling from north to south. When booking your tickets, pay close attention to arrival and departure times. On many occasions, I have had to literally run to my connecting flight because there was not enough time between flights. Always account for travel delays. On the opposite end, if you have too much time between flights you may want to make arrangements for your team to stay in a hotel. Staying overnight in an airport can be very difficult, and you do not want your team to be completely exhausted before you even arrive in-country for the mission.

You will also want to investigate which airport you will use to depart. Flying out of smaller regional airports can be very expensive, so driving to a larger international airport for departure may be cheaper for you and your team. If that is the case, you will have to make arrangements to get to this airport. Will you charter a bus for the whole team or ask each team member to meet at the airport?

Ministry materials. You have already determined what your ministry will be and when and how you will do it. Now, you and your leadership will need to determine what materials your team needs to make the mission a success. For example, if you are going to conduct a vacation Bible school for children in a third world country, you will need to purchase and pack the resources needed. Many of the things that we can easily purchase in the United States are hard to come by in other countries. Ask yourself how much will these materials cost. Collecting necessary items can be a great way to get your team involved in the preparation. Many churches, individuals, and even businesses are eager to donate toys, school supplies, clothes, medicines, Bibles, and other supplies. How will you get the materials to the field? It may be possible to pack materials in your team's suitcases. However, recent airline restrictions on the number of bags allowed and the weight requirement for each bag may cause you to consider other options. These may involve sending materials ahead of the team by airfreight or ship container.

What other materials are needed that can be purchased in-country? Obviously, a construction team cannot pack all the needed building supplies, and will have to coordinate beforehand to obtain everything they need to build from the destination itself. If you plan to hold a VBS, will you need to feed the children who come? Most likely, your missionary on the ground will need to make the arrangements for the food and you may need to wire-transfer the funds.

Shots and vaccines. Check with the Centers for Disease Control (CDC) or your local health department to find out what shots and medicines your team will need to travel to your destination. Be cautious about just checking the Internet for travel information. The CDC, your local health department, or your personal doctor will have more updated information about any recent health alerts on the ground in the country. If you must get several shots before traveling, inform your team not to get them all at once. We have had several team members get very sick from the vaccines because they had so many in one visit. If you are traveling to a third world country, be prepared to take anti-malaria medications before, during, and after the mission.

Emergency and insurance. In case of an emergency, how will you be contacted? Technology today makes it much easier to keep in touch with home than even a few years ago. Will you need a satellite phone? Will there be Internet access? Do you need to purchase a cell phone when you arrive? From what company will you purchase travel insurance for each team member? There are several good organizations that provide short-term medical coverage for individuals traveling. Do not wait for an emergency to find out the importance of being covered in another country. Accidents do happen, and you must be prepared for them ahead of time. Do any of the team members have a medical condition that would make the mission more difficult for both the individual and the team? If hiking or long-distance walking is required, the trip may not be suitable for someone with poor knees, severe asthma, or other severe conditions. What medicines should you take with you in case a team member gets sick?

Passports and visas. If a team member does not yet own a passport, have him or her apply for one as soon as possible. It can take six to eight weeks to receive your passport. Also be sure that you have at least four blank pages in the back of your passport if you have one. The requirement for blank pages varies from country to country, and some airlines will not let you board the plane unless your passport meets this requirement. Countries also vary on whether you will need a visa is to enter the country and whether or not you need to apply for one in advance. Investigate these details so you won't be caught off guard. It is also a good idea to make several photocopies of your passport in the event that it gets lost or stolen. Each team member should leave a copy at home and give a copy to the team leader.

Returning home. Every team member may have been trained and prepared for the trip, but it is also necessary to prepare them for the return home. Sometimes it is difficult for people to go back to work or school, daily responsibilities, and the status quo. Their minds and hearts remain with the precious people to whom they ministered on their mission. They leave a country of poverty only to return to a country with plenty. Be sensitive to this reverse culture shock and help your team make this difficult transition. This is where you will see God make the greatest impact on your people. Individuals who participate in a short-term mission often come home with a deeper love for Jesus Christ and a greater compassion for the world. Encourage them not to return to life as usual but to use this experience to change the way they share the gospel.

Preparing for the Unexpected

Anyone who has been involved in volunteer missions knows that situations can change very quickly. A bus breakdown, a lost passport, sickness, theft, flight cancellations, and any number of other things can change the mission itinerary. I have a pastor friend who was returning from Africa with his mission team when a massive snowstorm hit. They were in London's Heathrow airport at the time trying to catch a flight to Washington, DC. The snowstorm covered much of that part of Europe and shut down airports everywhere. My friend had no alternative than to get hotel rooms for all of his team members. They ended up being stranded for several days. This was a great strain on his mission budget, as he had to pay the extra bills due to the delay.

The best way to prepare for the unexpected is to expect it! Things will rarely work out in the exact manner you have planned. When they don't, do not panic. Remember that you are in God's hands. When things start to spin out of control, remember that you never had anything under your control in the first place. Our sovereign

Lord can be trusted to lead you and your team through difficulties and setbacks. We always remind our teams to be flexible at all times. Our Lord has promised to work on our behalf for our good and for His glory (Romans 8:28).

There have been times when the Lord has used what I thought was a roadblock to open up other doors for ministry. The Lord has given us many divine appointments that we would have missed without delays and changes in plans. Keep looking for opportunities for ministry during times of unexpected events.

Here are some considerations to keep in mind when the unexpected happens.

1. Get the team in a safe location. Our most common delays in third world countries are vehicle breakdowns. In these cases, team members need to be clear of the highway or other locations where they could be injured.
2. Stay as a group. If things begin to go wrong, there is safety in numbers.
3. The team leader should take charge of the situation. When the leader does not lead through the crisis, the team will begin to panic and pull apart. Tell the team exactly what has happened and what you need them to do. This is not the time for everyone to take matters into their own hands.
4. If you have a cell phone, promptly call those who need to be informed about your situation.
5. Keep emergency cash available for unexpected situations.
6. Have a first aid kit accessible at all times and make sure it is well—stocked.

Managing Logistics

7. Be resourceful. Look for people around you who may be able to help your situation, such as a police officer, airport security, etc.
8. Know where the American Embassy is located and how to contact it.
9. Remember: flexibility, flexibility, flexibility!
10. Finally, "Rejoice always, pray without ceasing, in everything give thanks; for this is the will of God in Christ Jesus for you" (1 Thessalonians 5:16-17).

Chapter Seven
Spiritual Preparation

"All of my life I have waited to hear this message. What took you so long to get here?"
~ An elderly Kenyan man after hearing the gospel for the first time.

I have encountered many people over the years who have expressed an interest in taking a mission trip. Conversations with some of these people have revealed that the true nature of their interest was not in the gospel but in adventure, travel, or sightseeing. Once while preparing to take a team to Africa, I received a call from someone who wanted to go along. "Will we get to see exotic animals?" she asked. "Will we get to see many of the sights? Oh, and I must have a hot shower. Can you guarantee that I will have a hot shower every day?" It quickly became apparent that her desire was not proclaiming the gospel, but meeting her own personal agenda.

We must remember to stress to our people that a mission trip is a **mission trip**. The objective of the mission is not sightseeing, adventure, taking a vacation, or even social work. The primary directive is the undiluted and unapologetic proclamation of the forgiveness of sins found in Jesus Christ alone! Certainly there may be passing opportunities to see historical places, meet interesting people, and take in breathtaking sights. These are all possible to do while the team travels, but they are never the focus of the trip. Those who are planning to participate in the mission need to be preparing themselves as ambassadors of our Lord Jesus Christ. Our mission is real and is not to be taken lightly.

So how does a person begin the spiritual preparation for a mission? First, each person must be certain of his or her salvation and personal relationship with Jesus. That should go without saying, but I have met people on trips who were still uncertain about their own salvation. It is extremely difficult to offer someone else the message of eternal life if you are not even convinced you possess it yourself. Make it a priority to determine that every team member is saved and certain.

Secondly, each team member should be growing in his or her relationship with Jesus Christ. They should be connected and involved in a local New Testament church. There needs to be evidence that the person is pursuing Bible study as well as prayer and fellowship with other believers. A team member who is not right in his or her relationship with God here will have a difficult time expressing His love to people living there.

Thirdly, each team member should exhibit a Christlike attitude in relationships with other people. We are not looking for spiritual perfection or none of us would qualify for the mission. However, we are looking for people whose daily lives reflect the love of God and the desire to please Him. People who are difficult to get along with, who have a hard time taking instructions from others, or who have a "short fuse" can compromise the whole mission. The people you have been sent to minister to will quickly detect if there is anger, arrogance, selfishness, or other ungodly attitudes among the team members. The very nature of a mission trip can prove to be stressful and difficult. When the pressures involved in the work begin to squeeze us, we want to make sure that the compassion of our Savior spills out. As the expression goes, "Whatever is down in the well comes up in the bucket."

Fourthly, each team member should enlist a group of praying people to support him or her. The very moment the church begins to be involved in a mission, the Devil will fight against it. I cannot stress enough the importance of having a group of prayer warriors undergirding the mission. When we take the gospel to the nations, we are invading the Enemy's territory, and he will not give it up without a fight. Scripture reminds us how to fight this battle in Ephesians 6.

> Put on the whole armor of God, that you may be able to stand against the wiles of the devil. For we do not wrestle against flesh and blood, but against principalities, against powers, against the rulers of the darkness of this age, against spiritual hosts of wickedness in the heavenly places. Therefore take up the whole armor of God, that you may be able to withstand in the evil day, and having done all, to stand. Stand therefore, having girded your waist with truth, having put on the breastplate of righteousness, and having shod your feet with the preparation of the gospel of peace; above all, taking the shield of faith with which you will be able to quench all the fiery darts of the wicked one. And take the helmet of salvation, and the sword of the Spirit, which is the word of God; praying always with all prayer and supplication in the Spirit, being watchful to this end with all perseverance and supplication for all the saints—and for me, that utterance may be given to me, that I may open my mouth boldly to make known the mystery of the gospel. (Ephesians 6:11-19)

Spiritual Preparation

I have come to believe that those preparing for a mission trip become the particular target of the Devil's fiery arrows. I can almost always expect to run into opposition and trouble just before, during, or right after a mission. By opposition I mean unforeseen situations, events, and circumstances that disrupt me, my family, or our team members.

While I was in Nepal, the IRS froze our family's bank account, making it impossible for my wife to get food and provisions. The IRS had made a mistake that they later corrected but not before causing us deep worry and concern while I was thousands of miles from home.

When my son, Jonathan, was a teenager, he was working with a mission in the jungles of Venezuela. At the same time, my wife and I were leading a mission in East Africa. Late one night, as we arrived back from a long day of ministry, we received an emergency phone call. The message we received said, "Your son has had an accident. He fell from a roof in the jungle and is now being flown back to the United States for emergency surgery. That is all we know." We did not know if his accident was life-threatening or how severe it was. We were in shock. All we could do was pray and trust in our sovereign God. It was not until the next day that we received more information about what had happened. We discovered that he had passed out while working on a missionary's roof. He fell from the roof and broke his arm (thankfully not his neck) in several places. He recovered quickly and we were soon reunited together at home.

Two weeks before leaving on a mission, my daughter, Joy, had a terrible reaction to some malaria medication she was taking. She had an extreme panic attack and ended up in the hospital in the middle of the night. The effects of that reaction affected her for many months.

One week before my wife, Janet, and I were leaving for Africa, we dined at a local seafood restaurant. When we got home, she had an anaphylactic reaction to the shellfish she had eaten (We had no idea she was allergic.). Her tongue and throat swelled until she could no longer breathe. The paramedics had to transport her to the hospital where we spent a long, sleepless night until the attack ended. The next week we were in the African bush sharing the gospel.

Another time, I was on my way to the airport to catch a flight to Japan, when the vehicle in front of me hit a large block of wood lying in the street. The block suddenly became a missile as it catapulted into the air. At sixty miles per hour, the wood block crashed through my windshield not far from my head and threw shattered glass into my face. I picked pieces of glass out of my hair for days. Not only had the Lord prevented the block of wood from smashing into my face, He also kept any glass from getting into my eyes. I made it to the airport in one piece and departed for Japan.

Two weeks before I was to leave for Korea, I had a sudden blackout spell. I have had never passed out before and haven't since. Thankfully my wife was with me and was able to get me to the emergency room. I spent two days in the hospital and went through a battery of tests that never showed a sign of trouble in my body. Two weeks later I was in Korea preaching the gospel of Jesus Christ and seeing God work in the hearts of many people.

One evening I was on the phone with my daughter who was spending the summer in East Africa. While we were talking, thousands of miles apart, she began to have an allergic reaction to yet another type of medication. She said, "Dad, I don't feel right." Her lips and her tongue swelled, and her windpipe began to close. Our dear Ugandan pastor, Godfrey, rushed her through the city trying to find a doctor or nurse who could help her. My wife and I listened helplessly over the phone as she gasped for breath. We could only hope and pray that a doctor could be found in time (This is not an easy task in a third world country in the middle of the night).

Spiritual Preparation

After several attempts and dead ends, they located a doctor who immediately began to treat her, literally saving her life.

Several years ago, I was a part of a team discreetly distributing Bibles in a Muslim country. Although what we were doing was not illegal in that country, the authorities frowned upon it. Things were going well that week and the Lord was working. I was staying with a precious missionary couple who were serving in that country "under the radar." One night, at about three o'clock in the morning, I walked to the bathroom, which was down the hall from my bedroom. As I made my way down the hallway, I was suddenly seized by severe pain in my lower back. It felt as if I was in a vise grip and being pressed harder and harder. I cried out in pain and fell to the floor, waking up the entire family.

Immediately this couple rushed into the hallway and found me collapsed on the floor. They gently lifted me to my feet and carried me back to my bed. The pain continued, and I felt as if some strange force was crushing me. My mind raced, trying to figure out why I was having such pain. I had not previously had trouble with my back. In fact, I had never experienced anything like it before (and haven't since).

This dear missionary husband, with deep spiritual insight, said, "We don't want to alarm you, but we have seen this kind of thing many times before. I believe that we are involved in spiritual warfare this week, and this is the attack of the Enemy. May we pray for you?"

I urgently agreed as I lay there in excruciating pain. This dear brother began to pray over me, and as he prayed I felt my arm getting wet. I opened my eyes to see tears streaming down the face of this missionary. The tears were dripping off his chin and onto my arm. While we continued to cry out to God, the pain suddenly subsided. The pressure on my back released, as though someone had taken me out of the vise.

The next morning I felt great and did not have the slightest bit of pain or soreness. When I returned home after the mission, I met with my doctor and related the story. Could it have been a severe muscle spasm or kidney stones, I asked. He ordered a series of tests, which revealed nothing. There were no signs of stress or scar tissue. My doctor (who is also a believer) concurred with my missionary friend that it must have been an attack from the enemy to hinder the work of proclaiming the gospel. We were in enemy territory shining the light of Jesus Christ in a very dark land. I am so glad the Word of God reminds us "He who is in you is greater than he who is in the world" (1 John 4:4).

I share these events with you not to create fear or to sound sensational. I share these events as a reminder that we are involved in a spiritual battle for the souls of humanity. We are "light bearers" shining the light of Jesus Christ into darkened areas of our world. God's glorious light dispels the darkness but also stirs up the Prince of Darkness as we invade his territory. When the apostle Paul was proclaiming the gospel to the people of Corinth he said, "For a great and effective door has opened to me, and there are many adversaries" (1 Corinthians 16:9).

We find a great battle cry in 2 Corinthians 4.

> But even if our gospel is veiled, it is veiled to those who are perishing, whose minds the god of this age has blinded, who do not believe, lest the light of the gospel of the glory of Christ, who is the image of God, should shine on them. For we do not preach ourselves, but Christ Jesus the Lord, and ourselves your bondservants for Jesus' sake. For it is God who commanded light to shine out of darkness, who has shone in our hearts to give the light of the knowledge of the glory of God in the face of Jesus Christ. (2 Corinthians 4:3-6)

Spiritual battles must be fought with spiritual weapons. "For the weapons of our warfare are not carnal but mighty in God for pulling down strongholds, casting down arguments and every high thing that exalts itself against the knowledge of God, bringing every thought into captivity to the obedience of Christ" (2 Corinthians 10:4-5). This spiritual battle is very real, and the enemy is ready to strike. It is absolutely essential that we saturate every trip in prayer and have a group of prayer warriors who will pray for the work to be done and for the protection of the workers.

As you spiritually prepare yourself and your team for a mission across the globe, I encourage you to follow this prayer guide.

Pray for the people.

"The poor shall eat and be satisfied; Those who seek Him will praise the Lord. Let your heart live forever! All the ends of the world shall remember and turn to the Lord, and all the families of the nations shall worship before You" (Psalm 22:26-27).

Pray for the ministry of the gospel to bear fruit.

"Therefore, if anyone is in Christ, he is a new creation; old things have passed away; behold, all things have become new. Now all things are of God, who has reconciled us to Himself through Jesus Christ, and has given us the ministry of reconciliation, that is, that God was in Christ reconciling the world to Himself, not imputing their trespasses to them, and has committed to us the word of reconciliation. Now then, we are ambassadors for Christ, as though God were pleading through us: we implore you on Christ's behalf, be reconciled to God. For He made Him who knew no sin to be sin for us, that we might become the righteousness of God in Him" (2 Corinthians 5:17-21).

Pray for boldness.

"Praying always with all prayer and supplication in the Spirit, being watchful to this end with all perseverance and supplication for all the saints—and for me, that utterance may be given to me, that I may open my mouth boldly to make known the mystery of the gospel" (Ephesians 6:18-19).

Pray for physical protection.

"The Lord is your keeper; The Lord is your shade at your right hand. The sun shall not strike you by day, nor the moon by night. The Lord shall preserve you from all evil; He shall preserve your soul. The Lord shall preserve your going out and your coming in from this time forth, and even forevermore" (Psalm 121:5-8).

Pray for unity among the team, the missionaries, and the church.

"I, therefore, the prisoner of the Lord, beseech you to walk worthy of the calling with which you were called, with all lowliness and gentleness, with longsuffering, bearing with one another in love, endeavoring to keep the unity of the Spirit in the bond of peace. There is one body and one Spirit, just as you were called in one hope of your calling; one Lord, one faith, one baptism; one God and Father of all, who is above all, and through all, and in all" (Ephesians 4:1-6).

Pray for the spiritual growth of each team member as well as new converts.

"Grow in the grace and knowledge of our Lord and Savior Jesus Christ. To Him be the glory both now and forever. Amen" (2 Peter 3:18).

Pray for a genuine love for the people to whom you will minister.

"We loved you so much that we were delighted to share with you not only the gospel of God but our lives as well, because you had become so dear to us" (1 Thessalonians 2:8).

Pray for a genuine compassion to help those in need.

"Open your mouth, judge righteously, defend the rights of the poor and needy" (Proverbs 31:9).

Pray for each team member to have the heart of a servant.

"Whoever desires to become great among you shall be your servant. And whoever of you desires to be first shall be slave of all. For even the Son of Man did not come to be served, but to serve, and to give His life a ransom for many" (Mark 10:43-45).

Chapter Eight
A Movement among Us

"The Gospel is only good news if it gets there in time."
~ Carl F.H. Henry

One hundred years ago, the concept of short-term missions was unheard of. Churches would not have even considered sending teams of lay people to faraway places for a very short period of time. The sheer number of obstacles would have made it impossible to participate in short-term mission involvement.

In the early 1900s there was a great worldwide missionary movement. Men and women sold everything they had, packed up their families, and took the gospel to the remotest places of the earth. However, the journey involved was nothing like it is today. It would have taken a missionary family months to travel to their destination. First, they had to take a dangerous voyage across thousands of miles of open sea. Once they reached land, there was still the difficulty of land travel. They had to use horse-drawn wagons and carts to find their way through unmarked territory and treacherous terrain. In some places the only way to travel was by foot.

Missionary biographies reveal the many hardships these men and women had to endure just to get to their fields of service. In some cases the missionaries never arrived at all. Some died en route to their assignment due to shipwreck, disease, hostile natives, and governments who opposed the gospel of Jesus Christ.

Things have drastically changed in our world over the last century. Today we can make that same journey within a single day. The obstacles and barriers have largely been removed by modern travel, technology, health care, and contemporary mission strategies.

The Age of Instant Communication

Satellites, GPS, jet airlines, advanced road systems, helicopters and other modern forms of transportation make it possible to reach areas of the planet that were once inaccessible. Imagine having to wait months for a letter to reach its destination. On my recent trip to Venezuela I was sending tweets from the middle of the Amazon jungle! A few years ago, that would have meant I was talking to the birds. Technology is forever changing, and it now takes only a fraction of a second to send a message to someone across the globe, not months. Information is acquired, contacts are made, and plans are established in no time at all.

Changes in Mission Strategy

Mission agencies and churches once viewed the professionally trained missionary as the only one who could carry out God's call to the nations. Untrained laypeople were viewed as inadequate, unnecessary, and a hindrance. Now we have discovered the great usefulness of volunteers working beside the missionary in his or her place of service. Projects that would have taken the lone missionary weeks or months to complete can now be accomplished much more quickly with the aid of volunteer mission teams. Volunteer teams now help build structures, offer medical care, conduct church leader training, and present the gospel in schools, villages, prisons, and just about anywhere. Some missionaries use volunteer teams as a major part of their mission strategy. The short-term mission has become a major player in the game plan of reaching this world for Christ.

The English Language

As technology is advancing, the planet is getting smaller. In many ways our world has become a global community without borders. English has become the accepted universal language of the world. Even developing countries have made learning English an important part of their educational process. You can go to virtually any country in the world and find people speaking English. In fact, there are so many people who want to learn English that many missionaries use teaching English as a platform for the gospel. In most places I travel, people are eager to try their English skills with me. Talking with them presents a very natural way to share the message of Jesus Christ and build new friendships.

Health care

I have read the heartbreaking accounts of missionaries who died on their mission field due to disease and sickness. The missionary families of the 1900s were regularly confronted with health crises. Many of them lost children and spouses to diseases that can be easily and quickly cured today. The use of antibiotics and vaccines and improved hygiene practices have made traveling abroad much safer for the missionary as well as the short-term volunteer. For example, we now know how to prevent malaria, yellow fever, cholera, hepatitis, typhoid, and other illnesses that would have prevented a volunteer from taking the gospel to a foreign land in the twentieth century. The risks have been greatly reduced, and volunteers can feel much safer about their health when planning a mission.

The DNA of a Mission-Minded Church

It takes more than just an occasional mission trip to transform a church into a world-focused, mission-minded body of Christ. Accomplishing this transformation involves a strategy and a vision to keep the needs of the world before our people. Unless a church makes an intentional effort to focus on missions, missions will eventually fade into the background. The very nature of keeping the church machinery operating will overshadow the pressing needs of a world without Jesus Christ. What vision will your church adopt in order to increase its passion for the gospel and involvement in world missions? What does a missional strategy look like for a church that wants to keep a lost world in focus?

First, adopt a people group or an international city and make it the object of your church's prayer life. Often the people group a church adopts will be one that already has a missionary on the ground. This allows you to pray for, serve, and support the people and the missionary living there and serving them. On the other hand, perhaps the area or people you choose has no missionary, and your commitment to pray for that people or area may lead a full-time missionary to invest there long-term.

Second, be specific and intentional about praying for your missionaries and your missional efforts. How many times in a prayer service have you heard someone pray, "Lord please bless all of the missionaries who are working all over the world. Protect them and use them for Your glory. Amen"? We should make our prayer times more focused on the names, the groups of people, and the types of ministry our missionaries are involved in helping. Instead of praying a general prayer for the missionaries all over the world, pray for a specific missionary.

For example:

> Father, we remember the Johnson family today as they serve you in Japan. Open the hearts of the Japanese people to the gospel of Jesus Christ. Enable them to be greatly used of You as they plant a new church in Tokyo this year. Send them volunteers who will help them in canvassing the apartment complexes where the church will be located. Allow the Johnsons to be fully encouraged in their work. Fill them with your Spirit. Change lives and draw people to Yourself for Your glory. Amen!

When our people begin hearing about and praying for specific needs of specific missionaries in specific places, they can better see God's specific purpose for this world.

Third, establish communication between the missionaries and your church. Post their newsletters and other correspondence where church members can read them. Mention to the congregation, Sunday school classes, or small groups any special needs or praise reports from the missionary. Give frequent updates on how God is working. To use the Johnson family as an example again: "We rejoice today with the Johnson family in Japan that they have secured a meeting place for the new church plant!" The key is to keep the mission in front of your people. If someone thinks you focus too much on missions, you are doing something right.

Fourth, encourage each Sunday school class or small group to meet a need for your missionary. You could say, "The Johnson family needs twelve sewing machines for their ministry to widows. Our small group is committing to raise the funds for them." When the members of your church begin to invest their time and money, they will begin to invest their hearts as well.

Fifth, plan a missions fair or missions conference. Take time out of your church's schedule each year to place a special emphasis on missions, both locally and globally. This is a great opportunity to present outreach opportunities to your people and provide information about your upcoming short-term mission trips. I know of churches that have a passport application table. Anyone can go there to begin the process of applying for his or her passport. After all, how can we tell God we are willing to go if we are not able to go? Encourage every church member to have an updated passport. Ask missionaries who are home on furlough to visit your church during your mission week and give a report of what God is doing. It is one thing to watch a video or read a report, but it is another thing entirely to hear from the missionary who has personally witnessed God working.

Finally, develop a budget that puts God's mission at the center of your church's map. How can you expect your people to invest into God's work around the world, if the church infrastructure does not? Set aside a special fund to aid those going on a trip, budget to send your church staff on at least one trip every year, or commit to financially supporting at least one full-time missionary. Some new church models encourage churches to designate 50 percent of their annual budget toward global missions and church planting. Make missions a key priority in your church, not an afterthought.

It is exciting to watch God begin to transform churches that have never been directly involved in missions. The size of the congregation does not matter. Every church, regardless of size, location, budget, or influence, can become a world-focused church. Will you join the great God of the universe in His mission of redeeming souls from every tribe, tongue, culture, and class? Will you trust Him to use whatever gifts, resources, and abilities found in your own local church to be a part of His plan of reaching the nations? May God give to you the very essence of Ephesians 3:20-21. "Now to Him who is able to do exceedingly abundantly above all that we ask or think, according to the power that works in us, to Him be glory in the church [your church] by Christ Jesus to all generations, forever and ever. Amen."

Spiritual Awakening

There is a definite move of God's Spirit in the lives of many of His people. Churches and individuals are beginning to take the Great Commission seriously. New waves of volunteers are coming forth to take part in God's worldwide mission. This is evidenced by the thousands of students who are signing up to use their summer vacations for a mission cause. This can also be seen in the number of retired people who see volunteer missions as a fulfilling way to use their talents, wisdom, time, and money to serve the Lord.

Every day we draw closer to the return of our Lord Jesus and the end of these days of grace. My own personal prayer has been that God would allow me to be a part of a great "last days harvest" of souls. These are days of great opportunity. I am convinced that our Lord is saying to His church today what He said to the church of Philadelphia. "I have set before you an open door, and no one can shut it" (Revelation 3:8). The question that we must keep asking ourselves is, "How long will the Lord allow the doors to remain open?" In my estimation, God has been stirring His church with a renewed sense of urgency. As the great theologian Carl F.H. Henry said, "The Gospel is only good news if it gets there in time."

May God replace our gospel hoarding with a great urgency to deliver His message to this lost, hopeless world. May He continue to awaken His church to the needs of 2.4 billion people who have yet to hear the good news of forgiveness and eternal life. Let church history record that this was the greatest time of global harvest since the days of Pentecost! Amen and amen.

World Reach Partnerships

It is our desire to see every local church directly involved in international missions, equipping and sending both full-time missionaries and short-term teams. World Reach Partnerships exists to partner with your local church in its global mission efforts. With more than twenty years experience in over forty countries, we partner closely with foreign churches and the missionaries on the ground, seeking to make the most of a short time of ministry. Let us be a part of your next mission trip. Assemble your team and choose your location. We will do everything else. We will plan the trip, train the team, and lead the mission, so you can focus on doing ministry. Please contact us for more information about partnering with us around the world.

World Reach Partnerships
P.O. Box 582, Blue Ridge, VA 24064
(540) 521-4508
worldreachpartners.org

Notes

1 Hadaway, Kirk and Penny Marler. *Journal for Scientific Study of Religion* 44, no. 3 (September 2005): 307-322
2 *Harper San Francisco Book Catalog* (May-August 2007): 15
3 Ibid
4 2011-2012 Data Tables. *The Association of Theological Schools.* www.ats.edu. Accessed June 28, 2012.
5 Report Examines the State of Mainline Protestant Churches. Posted December 7, 2009. *The Barna Group of Ventura, California.* www.barna.org. Accessed June 28, 2012.
6 Dempsey-Colson, Margaret. "Florida Baptists celebrate the anniversary of Haiti missions partnership." Posted November 22, 2010. *Florida Baptist Witness.* www.gofbw.com. Accessed June 28, 2012.
7 Southern Baptist Convention. "Missions Work." www.sbc.net. Accessed June 28, 2012

CPSIA information can be obtained at www.ICGtesting.com
Printed in the USA
BVOW011628130812

297749BV00001B/2/P

9 781449 759773